Australia's
PARROTS

Above: Sulphur-crested cockatoo, *Cacatua galerita* (see page 27).
Left: The eclectus parrot, *Eclectus roratus* (see page 10).

Photography by Ken Stepnell
&
Text by Jane Dalby

C&A CHILD & ASSOCIATES
AN ALL-AUSTRALIAN PUBLISHER

Ken Stepnell, renowned as one of Australia's leading photographers of our natural wonders, travels over 100 000 kilometres annually continually searching for new subjects to enhance his superb photographic library.

His eye for detail has enabled readers to appreciate the beauty and variety of our natural resources through many publications. His photographs show the delicate balance of nature and the need to preserve our heritage.

His other book s include *Australian Birds, Australia's Native Flowers* and *Australian Animals.*

Jane Dalby was encouraged to take an interest in natural history by her parents and grandparents. She obtained a BA in Biology and Ecology from Macquarie University. She is now a Technical Officer at the National Herbarium at the Botanic Gardens, Sydney, New South Wales. This involves looking after the collection of dried plants used in research and identification.

Her great interest in birds has developed over the last four or five years and has led to an extensive study of their habits and features. Her first book *Australian Birds* was published in 1986.

Above: Gang gang cockatoos, *Callocephalon fimbriatum* (see page 14).

Front cover: Major Mitchell cockatoo, *Cacatua leadbeateri* (see pages 28-9).
Endpapers: Galahs, *Cacatua roseicapilla* (see page 13).
Back cover: Princess parrot, *Polytelis alexandrae* (see pages 37-8).

Published by Child & Associates Publishing Pty Ltd
5 Skyline Place, Frenchs Forest, NSW, Australia, 2086
A wholly owned Australian publishing company
This book has been edited, designed
and typeset in Australia by the Publisher
First Edition 1988
Photographs © Ken Stepnell 1988
Text © Jane Dalby 1988
Printed in Singapore by Kyodo-Shing
Loong Printing Industries Pte Ltd
Typesetting processed by Deblaere Typesetting Pty Ltd

All rights reserved. No part of this publication may be reproduced, stored in a retrieval system, or transmitted in any form or by any means, electronic, mechanical, photocopying, recording, or otherwise without the prior permission in writing of the publisher.

National Library of Australia
Cataloguing-in-Publication data

Dalby, Jane, 1945-
 Parrots.

 Includes index.
 ISBN 0 86777 356 1.

 1. Parrots. 2. Birds — Australia. 3. Parrots —
Pictorial works. 4. Birds — Australia — Pictorial
works. I. Stepnell, Kenneth, 1931- .
II. Title.

598'.71'0994

AUSTRALIAN PARROTS

Parrots, lorikeets and cockatoos belong to a most distinctive and easily recognisable group of birds, the order Psittaciformes, whose nearest relatives are believed to be the pigeons and doves.

Parrots are known to have been tamed and taught to mimic human speech since long before the time of Christ. Today, such birds as the South American macaws, African grey and peach-faced parrots, and of course many Australian cockatoos and parrots, are commonly kept as pets and aviary birds.

In Australia, a number of native species such as galahs, rosellas and lorikeets are also familiar town birds, frequenting urban bushland, parks and private gardens.

Today, about 330 species of parrot exist worldwide, the majority occurring in the southern hemisphere. Although the greatest number of species are to be found in the tropics, a significant number occur in the subtropical and temperate zones as well. The South American continent boasts the greatest number of species, although the parrots of this region are rather uniform in type. While fewer species occur in Australasia, parrots are well represented there, having evolved into a remarkable diversity of forms. Two striking groups, the lorikeets and the cockatoos, as well as a number of other species, are restricted to the region. Relatively few species of parrot are native to Africa, Asia and North America.

Australia, which is home to over fifty species, has long been known for its parrots. Dutch navigators in the seventeenth century, having seen flocks of cockatoos on the west coast of what is now known as Western Australia, named the country 'Terra Psittacorum' (Land of Parrots).

The first known drawing of an Australian parrot was of a female-plumaged red-tailed black cockatoo, made by Sydney Parkinson in 1770, on Captain Cook's first voyage to the Pacific. A live rainbow lorikeet taken back to Europe by Sir Joseph Banks was the first Australian parrot known to have been kept in captivity.

A flock of little corellas, *Cacatua sanguinea*. Such sights as this inspired the European navigators who first saw Australia to give it the name 'Terra Psittacorum' (Land of Parrots).

A rainbow lorikeet, *Trichoglossus haemadotus*, was the first Australian parrot taken back to Europe from Australia. Joseph Banks collected rainbow lorikeets on Cook's first voyage to the Pacific.

Features of Parrots

A number of striking features contribute to the characteristic appearance of parrots as a group. These include their often brilliant plumage colours, the naked or feathered cere, which bears the nostrils, the hooked bill and muscular tongue, and the zygodactylous feet, with two toes pointing forward and two backward.

Bill and Tongue

The strong hooked bill is one of the most easily recognisable features of all parrots. The bill grows continuously, at the same time being constantly worn away with use. Parrots use their bills not only for the obvious purposes of obtaining and breaking up food and for grooming, but also as an extra limb when climbing.

The upper mandible of most birds is attached directly to the skull and is immoveable from its fixed position. Parrots, however, have a complex hinge-like arrangement attaching the upper mandible to the skull. This gives them the capacity to open the beak wide and to exert considerable force with it. Anyone who has been bitten by a parrot will be able to vouch for the power of its bite! On the other hand, the bill can be used very gently when required, for example, for delicate tasks such as preening.

The crushing ability of the bill is used to open hard and woody fruits to extract the seeds which are a major component of the diet of most species. Other uses of the bill include removing insect larvae from galls or from under bark, and digging roots, corms etc. from the soil.

Some parrot species, such as the sulphur-crested cockatoo, Cacatua galerita, *are able to use a foot for holding food up to the bill while feeding.*

While the powerful hooked bill of the long-billed corella, Cacatua tenuirostris, *is adapted for crushing woody fruits and for digging for bulbs in the soil, it is also needed for delicate tasks such as grooming.*

Some species have evolved modifications of the bill which are related to the collection of particular foods. Long-billed corellas, for example, have a long upper mandible which is admirably suited for digging in the soil for bulbs and corms. Red-capped parrots also have an elongated upper mandible, which is adapted for extracting seed from the woody fruits of eucalypts, particularly those of the marri, a tree particularly favoured by this species.

The narrow protruding bills of lorikeets are adapted for probing blossom. In addition, the lorikeet group have evolved what is known as a 'brush' tongue. Numerous papillae at the tip of the tongue, which become erect during feeding, are an adaptation for taking up pollen and nectar from flowers. A similar tongue adaptation has evolved independently in the swift parrot, another specialist nectar and pollen feeder which is more closely related to the rosellas and bluebonnets than to the lorikeets.

By contrast, the cockatoos and other parrots have a thick and muscular though flexible tongue. They use the tongue, in conjunction with the beak, for manipulating and husking seeds, fruits and other food items.

Feet

Parrots have strong, short legs and feet with two toes pointing forward and two back. This arrangement enables them both to walk well on the ground, and also, often aided by the bill, to climb easily. In some species, for example, cockatoos and rosellas, the feet are often used, in conjunction with the bill and tongue, for holding and manipulating food. Preening and scratching are other functions requiring use of the feet.

In spite of the brilliant colours of birds such as this golden-mantled rosella, *Platycercus eximius* subsp. *cecilae*, they can be difficult to see when in their natural forest surroundings.

Colour

Feather structure and the presence of pigments are the factors involved in producing the colours of birds' plumage. The microscopic structure of the feathers of some species causes interference or backscattering of light. Iridescent colours, which change with viewing angle, are produced by interference, while backscattering gives rise to non-iridescent colours. Other non-iridescent colours are due to the presence of pigments or to a combination of structure and pigment. The brightest Australian parrots, such as lorikeets and rosellas are coloured mainly in green, red, blue and yellow, often with greens predominating. With colourings like these, the birds often appear very conspicuous when seen outside their normal surroundings. However, their colours are usually distributed in small broken patches, rather than in large areas of one colour. Thus, in the wild they can be very difficult to see in natural surroundings such as the vegetation of forest or woodland.

Species such as Bourke's parrot and the princess parrot are less brilliant, with plumage of lovely pastel shades of pink, blue and yellow. The regent parrot and blue-winged parrot are quite cryptically coloured, being predominantly yellow-green and olive respectively.

Cockatoos do not have the iridescent colours of other groups, as they lack the feather structure which produces these colours. The body and wing plumage of most cockatoos is basically plain black or white, with splashes or flecks of colour. The two exceptions to this are the galah, which is pink and grey, and the Major Mitchell cockatoo, which is pale pink and white, with salmon underwings.

The skin of soft parts of the body may also be coloured. The ceres of adult male budgerigars, for example, are a clear, bright blue. Galahs, depending on their subspecies, have either grey or deep pink skin around the eyes. In little corellas, this area is blue.

The most striking example of pigmented skin occurs in the palm cockatoo, *Probosciger aterrimus*. These birds have a black-tipped red tongue and red facial skin, which blushes even brighter when they are excited.

Bill colours also differ between species. The bill may be horn-coloured, grey, or black, as in cockatoos, ringnecks and rosellas; bright orange or red as in some lorikeets, or coral-coloured as in the king, red-winged, superb and princess parrots.

The lovely pastel shades of Bourke's parrot, *Neophema bourkii*, are quite a contrast to the brilliant colours of many other parrots.

The bloom or bluish sheen on the feathers of this red-tailed black cockatoo, *Calyptorhynchus magnificus*, is due to the presence of a powder which is produced by the breakdown of specialised down feathers and used by the bird for grooming its plumage.

Plumage

The most important contribution to a bird's appearance is made by the plumage, differences in which play a major role in species recognition. In addition, particular feathers have become adapted for display in some species. Good examples of this are the moveable crests of the cockatoos and the cockatiel.

Down feathers, which grow thickly under the contour feathers, provide insulation by trapping air against the skin. Parrots and several other groups of birds such as herons and woodswallows have a second type of down feather, known as 'powder down'. These feathers grow throughout the bird's life. The tips break down constantly, forming a fine powder which is used for grooming the feathers. It is this powder which gives the plumage its characteristic bloom, a feature which is particularly noticeable in the black cockatoos.

Sexual Differences

In some species of parrot, such as the little corella and the rainbow lorikeet, it is not possible to tell male and female apart visually. In many cases, however, the sexes are appreciably different in appearance. Amongst Australian parrots, the most striking instance of this phenomenon, which is known as sexual dimorphism, occurs in the eclectus parrot. The male and female of this species are so different in colouring that for many years they were thought to belong to different species. The male, which has an orange bill, is green with red flanks and wing lining, while the female has a black bill and is mostly red, with blue shoulders and breast band. Other parrots exhibit sexual dimorphism to varying degrees. The sexes are easily distinguished in such species as cockateils, black cockatoos and king parrots. In others, such as varied lorikeets and the blue-winged parrot, the differences are not as marked, the male being in general more brightly coloured than the female. The least obvious differences occur in species such as the pink cockatoo and galah, in which the sexes have similar plumage, but differ in eye colour, the male's iris being deep brown and that of the female being reddish pink.

The eclectus parrot, *Eclectus roratus*, inhabits the tropical rainforests of Cape York. This bird is a male—the female has a black bill and is mostly red, with blue shoulders and breast band.

Rainforest on Fraser Island, Queensland. Forests like this support such species as the king parrot, *Alisterus scapularis*, rosellas and lorikeets.

HABITATS

Parrots are able to exploit environments which provide their basic requirements for survival — suitable food, a water supply and nesting and roosting sites.

The Australian continent, which extends from the tropics to cool temperate zones, provides a great many suitable habitats for parrots. These include monsoon forests and rainforests, various types of woodland and grassland, tree-lined watercourses, farmlands, heath, saltmarsh and mangroves, to name but a few.

Some species of parrot have the ability to make use of a number of different habitats within their range. Lorikeets, for instance, are nomadic birds of the treetops, their movements being governed largely by the flowering of their food plants. Rainbow lorikeets have an extensive range down the eastern coast of Australia, extending to Tasmania and the south-east of South Australia. They frequent habitats ranging from tropical rainforest, sclerophyll forests and savannah woodland, to scrub and timbered watercourses and mangroves.

The blue-winged parrot of south-eastern Australia and Tasmania is another species which is able to make use of a number of different habitats. It frequents open forest, forested foothills and valleys, savannah woodland and grasslands, as well as coastal heathlands, sand dunes and saltmarsh.

The galah, one of Australia's most widespread and familiar cockatoos, was originally confined to the semi-arid and arid zones, in woodland, grassland and timber along streams. Galahs have been able to take advantage of habitat changes such as the clearing of timber and planting of grain and other crops. As a result, they have extended their range and are now to be found in areas where they were previously unknown, becoming agricultural pests in some places.

Arid environments such as the area south of Marble Bar in Western Australia are visited in favourable seasons by nomadic species like the budgerigar, *Melopsittacus undulatus*.

The hooded parrot, *Psephotus chrysopterygius* subsp. *dissimilis*, which occurs in the Northern Territory, nests in a chamber excavated in a termite mound.

Termite mounds in northern Australia. Both the golden-shouldered parrot, *Psephotus chrysopterygius*, and the hooded parrot require habitat such as this to provide nesting sites.

The swift parrot, *Lathamus discolor*, has evolved a narrow protruding bill and a brush-like tongue, adaptations for obtaining nectar and pollen from flowers.

Other, more specialised species have narrower habitat requirements, which effectively restrict their ranges. Golden-shouldered and hooded parrots occur in the Northern Territory and northern Queensland respectively. Because of their requirement for termite mounds as nesting sites, they are only to be found in open wooded habitats close to grassland where there are numerous terrestrial termite mounds present.

Rock parrots, *Neophema petrophila,* inhabit the coast and offshore islands of southern and south-western Australia. They are rarely to be seen more than a few hundred metres from the sea, in coastal sand dunes, saltmarsh and mangroves, or on small rocky islands. As these parrots only breed on islands, their range is restricted by the distribution of the coastal islands.

The seldom-seen night parrot, *Geopsittacus occidentalis,* occurs only in the arid centre of the continent. It is thought to be nomadic, and has been observed in salt lake and flood plain habitats, as well as in spinifex, when abundant seeding occurs after rain.

Ground parrots, *Pezoporus wallicus,* as their name suggests, are largely terrestrial, although they are able to fly well. They are rarely seen because of their dense habitat and their tendency to fly during daylight only if flushed from cover. Their optimum habitat is diverse heathland vegetation of 0.5 m to 1.5 m in height. This environment is dominated by sedges and heaths, scattered shrubs of banksia and teatree, and small eucalypts. Because of the destruction of this type of habitat by human activities, the ground parrot now has a distribution restricted to suitable areas scattered in coastal eastern Australia, from southeast Queensland to Victoria and Tasmania, its present stronghold.

Eclectus parrots, palm cockatoos, *Probosciger aterrimus,* and red-cheeked parrots, *Geoffroyus geoffroyi,* which occur in Australia on Cape York in Queensland, are birds of tropical rainforests. They have been prevented from extending their range to more southerly rainforests by the tract of savannah woodland to the south of Coen on Cape York Peninsula.

FEEDING

Apart from the lorikeets and the swift parrot, Australian parrots are primarily seed-eaters. However, a variety of other foods may be eaten also. These include fruits of various kinds, roots and bulbs, young shoots, flowers, pollen and nectar, and insects and their larvae.

Many Australian cockatoos and parrots are now known to include insects in their diet. Different species have been observed feeding on items identified as lerps and psillids, larvae of moths and other insects, and on the eggs of ants and plague locusts.

Some species have more specialised food requirements than others. Lorikeets, for example, forage in the treetops for pollen, nectar and fruit, but also take berries, seeds, insects and larvae.

Yellow-tailed black cockatoos feed mainly on the wood-boring larvae of moths and other insects, obtaining them from dead grass-tree spikes, dead wood and from the trunks of trees including eucalypts and wattles (*Acacia*). In part of their range, these cockatoos have been observed using extraordinary foraging behaviour. The bird first locates a hole containing a larva by listening at the tree trunk. It then proceeds to make itself a perch to work from. This it does by pulling a strip of wood from the tree trunk, so that it hinges just below the insect hole. The bird then stands on this perch and sets to work to dig out the larva.

The ground parrot, which inhabits heath and sedge lands, feeds mainly on the seeds of grasses, sedges and other herbaceous plants, as well as on young shoots. Favoured foods are the seeds of buttongrass, grasses and sedges.

The red-capped parrot of south-western Australia, also appropriately known as a 'hookbill', has a narrow, protruding bill, which is specialised for extracting seeds from the large, flask-shaped fruit of the marri, *Eucalyptus calophylla*. It also feeds on the seeds of other trees, including eucalypts and casuarinas, as well as on fruits, blossom, leaf buds and insects and larvae.

Since the advent of European man, cultivated plants have become a potential food source for birds. Hence parrots have come to be regarded as pests in some areas where commercial crops such as grains, soft fruits and nuts are grown. For example, galahs, sulphur-crested cockatoos and corellas are considered pests in grain-growing areas, where they cause damage by digging up sprouting seeds, or by eating the ripening crop or bagged grain. Others, such as king parrots and rosellas, attack fruit in apple, pear and peach orchards. In maize crops, they may eat the grain in the milky stage.

The elongated mandible of the red-capped parrot, *Purpureicephalus spurius*, is adapted for extracting seed from large eucalyptus fruits, particularly those of the marri, *Eucalyptus calophylla*.

Yellow-tailed black cockatoos, *Calyptorhynchus funereus*. Wood-boring larvae of insects, extracted from trees with their formidable bills, are an important part of the diet of this species.

The galah, *Cacatua roseicapilla*, is among Australia's most common and widespread parrots. Galahs have benefited from man's activities, such as clearing of timber and the planting of grain and oilseed crops.

COMMUNICATION

Birds have complex systems for conveying messages to each other, using combinations of calls, movements and plumage display. In this way, they co-ordinate the behaviour of members of the same species in such activities as feeding, flocking, breeding and reaction to predators.

Calls

Each species has a vocabulary of calls which are used in different situations. Thus alarm calls warning of danger are loud, but not directional, so that the bird giving the call is less likely to be located by a predator. Territorial calls are also loud, but are directional, as they are intended to identify the bird's territory. Contact calls are both quiet and non-directional, serving to maintain contact between members of the group.

The calls of Australian parrots are as varied as the birds themselves. The harsh, raucous cries of some of the cockatoos and the shrill screeching of lorikeets will be known to many people. The cheerful chattering of budgerigars is also a familiar sound the world over.

Not all of Australia's parrots have shrill or raucous calls, however. Some species, such as the king parrot and the eastern rosella, have rather musical notes among their repertoire of calls. Others make sounds which are quite unusual. The feeding call of gang gang cockatoos, for example, is a soft growling, while their contact call is a curious creaking sound.

Ground parrots give an ascending series of very high-pitched whistles which may be inaudible to some people. They usually call for short periods at dawn and dusk, as they fly between their roost trees and their daytime feeding areas in the heath.

Display

Palm cockatoos have recently been observed behaving in a most remarkable manner. Within their territory, they have a number of tree hollows which they visit regularly. Near these, they display by beating on a hollow trunk or limb, producing a drumming sound. This display is of particular interest because the drumming is produced with the aid of a tool, a type of behaviour exhibited by very few animals apart from man. The 'drumstick' may be a specially prepared stick, or the large woody fruit of the 'bushman's clothespeg', *Grevillea glauca*. This is held in the foot and beaten on a hollow limb. Drumming occurs early in the morning and evening and takes place most frequently during nest preparation and in the period just before the single young leaves the nest. Its functions appear to be to proclaim territory and perhaps to maintain the pair-bond.

Amongst parrots, courtship displays are usually quite uncomplicated, involving a series of simple actions. These include bowing, drooping and flicking of the wings, tail wagging, foot raising and dilation and contraction of the pupils. As mating approaches, the birds engage in close body contact such as mutual preening and courtship feeding, where the female is fed regurgitated food by the male, in the same manner as chicks are fed by the adults.

There is a marked difference in appearance between male and female gang gang cockatoos, *Callocephalon fimbriatum*. The head and crest of the male are a clear bright red, while those of the female are grey.

The pale-headed rosella, *Platycercus adscitus*, is closely related to both the eastern and northern rosellas. It is a lowland species which occurs in eastern Australia from the Cape York Peninsula south to the Clarence River in New South Wales.

These rosellas inhabit scrub and woodland, timbered watercourses and farmland adjoining these areas. They are usually observed in pairs or small parties, often feeding on or near the ground.

(Right)

The northern rosella, *Platycercus venustus*, is a handsome bird, with its black cap, white cheek patches and blue shoulders and tail. Its breast feathers are pale yellow edged with black and the undertail coverts are red. Its range is in northern Australia from the Kimberley region to far north-western Queensland. It is an uncommon bird and is usually seen in pairs or small groups of six to eight birds.

The golden-mantled rosella, *Platycercus eximius* subsp. *cecilae*, is a subspecies of the eastern rosella, occurring from south-eastern Queensland to the Hunter River valley in New South Wales. It is distinguished from the eastern rosella by its darker red head and breast, and by its back feathers, the margins of which are broader and gold in colour, rather than yellowish green.

Immature golden-mantled rosellas do not reach adult colouring until they are at least one year old. Unless a second brood is raised, the young birds remain with the parents in a family group.

(Left)

Eastern rosellas usually nest in tree hollows, but may use a fence post or tree stump. The chicks are fed by the female until they are about ten days old, after which both parents share the feeding.

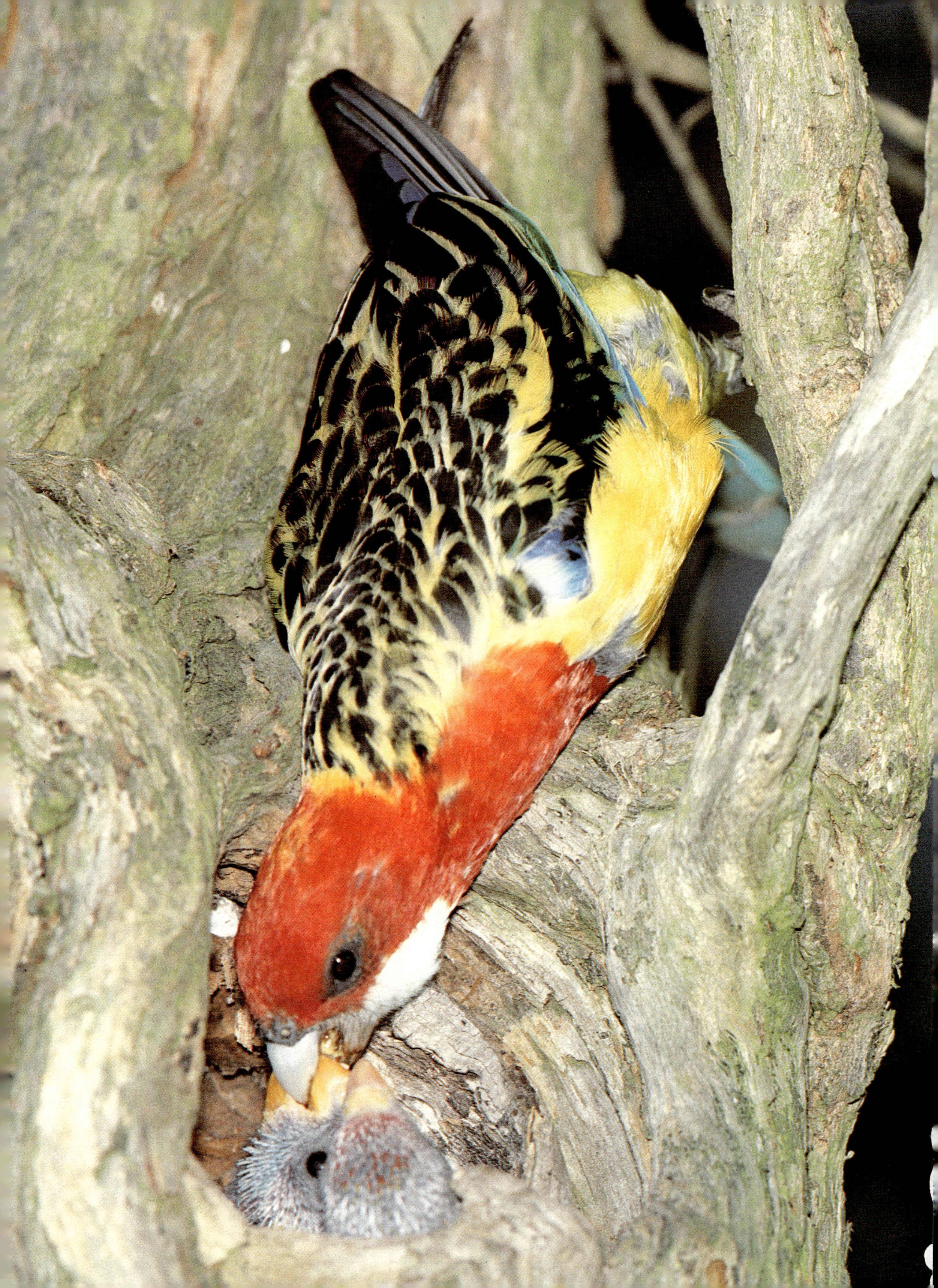

As their name implies, Adelaide rosellas, *Platycercus elegans* subsp. *adelaidae*, occur in the vicinity of Adelaide. They have a restricted distribution, from Clare in the north, to the tip of the Fleurieu Peninsula in the south.

Adelaide rosellas inhabit a variety of timbered environments. Adults are usually seen in pairs or in groups of up to five, while young birds may form wandering flocks.

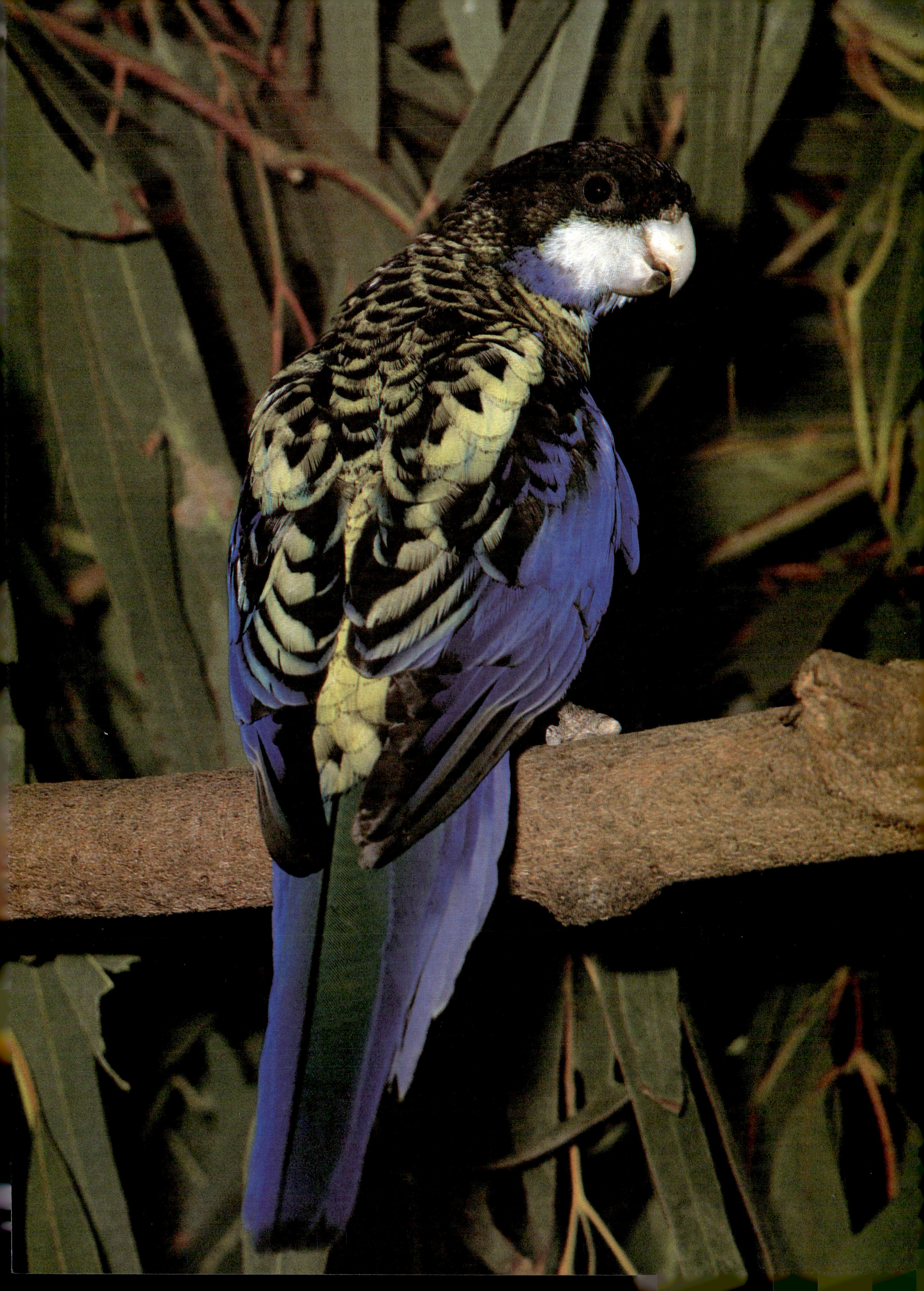

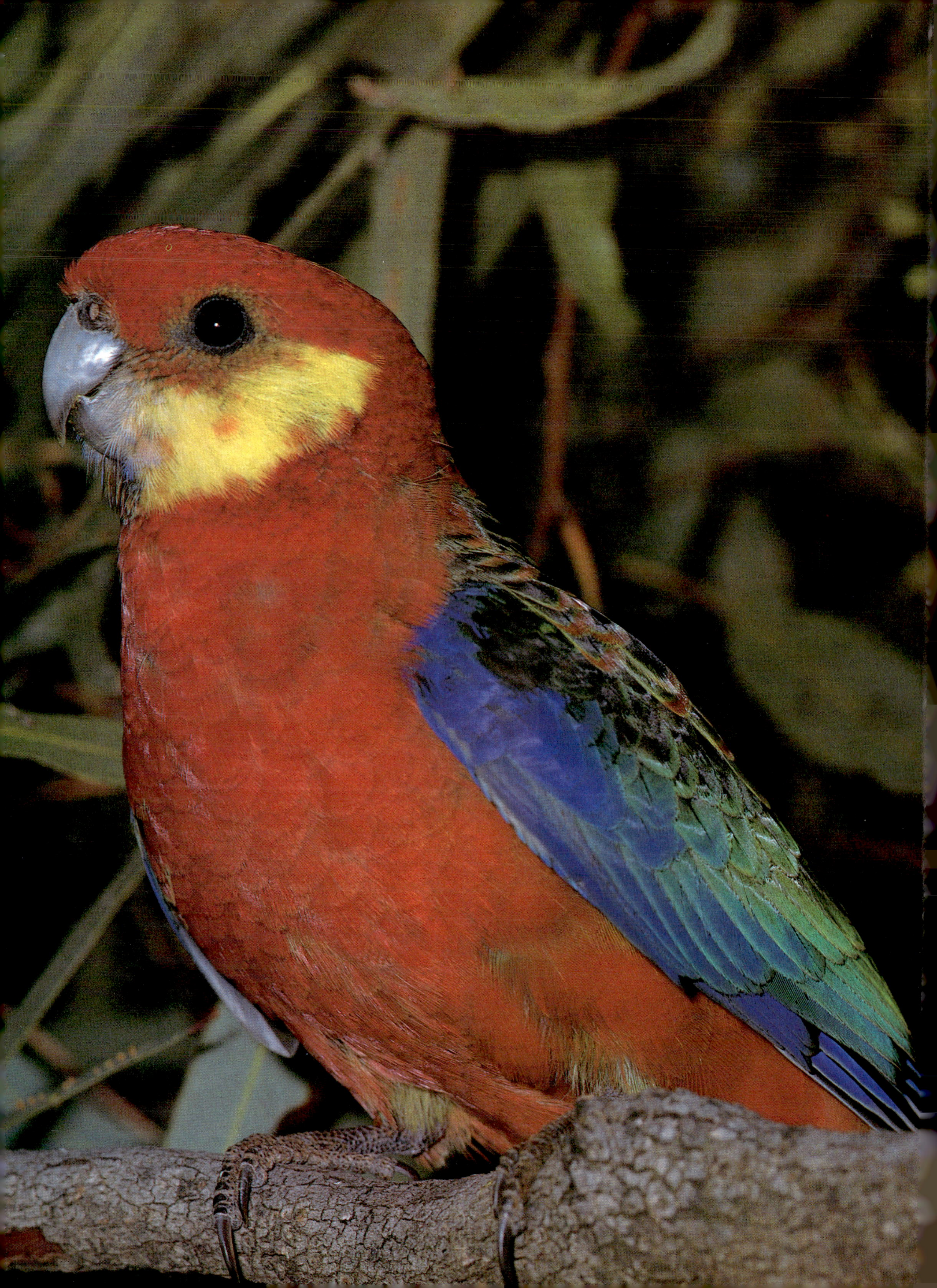

(Left)
The smallest of the rosellas, the western rosella, *Platycercus icterotis*, is confined to the south-west of Western Australia. It prefers open wooded habitats, including timbered watercourses, farmlands, orchards, roadsides and gardens.

Western rosellas are the only rosellas to have a yellow cheek patch. They also show quite marked sexual dimorphism, unlike others in the group. The female is generally darker than the male, with more green on the back, and blue edges to the outer tail feathers.

GENUS *PSEPHOTUS*, Grass Parrots

Parrots in this group, which includes the red-rumped parrot, bluebonnet and mulga parrot, are slim, medium-sized birds. Their backs are uniform in colour and they have long, graduated tails. All except the bluebonnet show marked sexual dimorphism. They are all ground-feeding seed-eaters.

One member of this group, the paradise parrot, is thought to be the only species of Australian parrot to have become extinct since European settlement.

Female red-rumped parrots are less colourful than the males, and do not have red on the rump. Nests are usually in a tree hole or hollow limb, often in a eucalypt close to water. More than one pair may nest in the same tree.

Red-rumped parrots, *Psephotus haematonotus*, are common in lightly timbered habitats throughout their range in south-eastern Australia. They are seldom far from water, and may be seen in woodlands, timber along watercourses, grassland, farms, mangroves and urban parks.

Grasslands, arid scrub and groves of trees scattered through sandy plains are the types of habitats favoured by mulga parrots, *Psephotus varius*. Their range in the interior of southern Australia extends from central and southern Western Australia to western New South Wales and southwestern Queensland. The male mulga parrot has a yellow frontal band and shoulder, and a scarlet patch across the belly and thighs. The female is generally green in colour, with red on the nape and shoulder.

Unlike other members of their genus, bluebonnets do not exhibit very pronounced sexual dimorphism. Members of this species are able to raise their blue frontal feathers to form a small crest, as shown in the photograph.

Red-vented bluebonnets, *Psephotus haemaatogaster* subsp. *haematorrhous*, are inland birds. Their range extends from Texas and Milmerran in southern Queensland to the black soil plains of the middle reaches of the Namoi and Gwydir Rivers of northern New South Wales.

(Right)

Male and female hooded parrots, *Psephotus chrysopterygius* subsp. *dissimilis*, are markedly different, the male with a rich yellow wing patch and a black cap, and the female coloured mainly in soft shades of green. These birds, which depend on terrestrial termite mounds for nesting sites, are restricted to the north-eastern region of the Northern Territory.

GENUS *NEOPHEMA*, Grass Parrots

Members of this genus are small ground-frequenting birds. They are graceful parrots which fly swiftly in a darting, zig-zag manner. Apart from Bourke's parrot, which is predominantly soft brown and pink, they all have plumage which is mainly olive green in colour.

(Left)

Bourke's parrot, *Neophema bourkii*, is a nomadic bird of the arid and semi-arid scrubs of the inland, particularly those dominated by mulga, *Acacia aneura*. Its range lies generally south of the Tropic of Capricorn, from south-western Queensland and the north-west of New South Wales, to Western Australia.

Blue-winged parrots, *Neophema chrysostoma*, are found in south-eastern Australia, including Tasmania and islands in Bass Strait. They frequent a variety of habitats, including open woodlands, lightly timbered grasslands, coastal scrub, heaths, coastal dunes and saltmarsh. This species breeds in Tasmania, southern Victoria and the south-east of South Australia. In autumn, most Tasmanian birds migrate north to spend winter on the mainland, returning in late spring. They may travel as far as eastern South Australia, north-western New South Wales and south-western Queensland.

Arid scrublands, particularly mallee and mulga with a spinifex understorey, are the habitats favoured by scarlet-chested parrots, *Neophema splendida*. Their range extends across the southern interior of Australia, from south-eastern Western Australia to the Flinders Ranges in South Australia, and south-western Queensland. The subdued plumage of the female is in sharp contrast to the bright colouring of the male shown in the photograph.

(Left)

Turquoise parrots, *Neophema pulchella*, were once abundant in New South Wales and Victoria, but their present distribution centres on south-east Queensland and northern New South Wales. Their range and numbers have declined, as a result of loss of suitable habitat, and also from illegal trapping for aviculture. The bird shown here is a female. The male has more blue on the face, is bright yellow underneath, and has a red flash on the wing.